MIDLOTHIAN PUBLIC LIBRARY

3 1614 00183 8342

W9-BHG-539

CREATE IT!

POP ART

Alix Wood

 Gareth Stevens
PUBLISHING

MIDLOTHIAN PUBLIC LIBRARY
14701 S. KENTON AVENUE
MIDLOTHIAN, IL 60445

Thank you to
Davina Cresswell
and Jemma Martin
for their help with
this book.

Please visit our website, **www.garethstevens.com**. For a free color catalog of all of our high-quality books, call toll free 1-800-542-2595 or fax 1-877-542-2596

Cataloging-in-Publication Data
Names: Wood, Alix.
Title: Pop art / Alix Wood.
Description: New York : Gareth Stevens Publishing, 2017. | Series: Create it! | Includes index.
Identifiers: ISBN 9781482450347 (pbk.) | ISBN 9781482450262 (library bound) | ISBN 9781482450255 (6 pack)
Subjects: LCSH: Pop art--Juvenile literature.
Classification: LCC N6494.P6 W66 2017| DDC 709.04'071--dc23

First Edition

Published in 2017 by
Gareth Stevens Publishing
111 East 14th Street, Suite 349
New York, NY 10003

Copyright © Alix Wood Books

Produced for Gareth Stevens by Alix Wood Books
Designed by Alix Wood
Editor: Eloise Macgregor

Photo credits: Cover, 1, 6 top, 7, 8 bottom, 9, 10 middle and bottom, 11, 12, 13, 14 bottom, 15, 16 bottom, 17, 19, 20, 21, 22, 23, 25 © Alix Wood; 3, 4, 5, 6 middle and bottom, 16 top, 24 bottom, 26, 27, 29 © Dollar Photo Club; 8 Allie Caulfield; 18 top © Raimond Spekking, CC-BY-SA-4.0 (via Wikimedia Commons); 18 bottom Bobak Ha'Eri; 24 top © Florent Bonnefoi; 28 © Kippelboy /Alix Wood; all remaining images are in the public domain

All rights reserved. No part of this book may be reproduced in any form without permission from the publisher, except by reviewer.

Printed in the United States of America
CPSIA compliance information: Batch #CS16GS: For further information contact
Gareth Stevens, New York, New York at 1-800-542-2595.

CONTENTS

WHAT IS POP ART?

Pop artists wanted to make art something everyone could enjoy. They took their **inspiration** from everyday life. Artists were inspired by images and objects seen all around them. They created art using things like pictures from advertising images or product labels. Pop art started in Britain in the 1950s, and became popular in the US in the 1960s and 1970s.

Pop art usually used bold and bright colors. Some pop artists got their inspiration from popular comic book pictures.

Meet a Pop Artist

Andy Warhol was famous for using images of **brands** in his art. One of his best known paintings was of a can of a well-known soup brand! He often **mass-produced** his art using printing techniques. He sometimes used well-known faces in his art. He created images of the singer Elvis Presley and film star, Marilyn Monroe.

TECHNIQUE TIPS

Andy Warhol often repeated the same image several times in his art. Some **art critics** didn't like his work. They didn't understand why he copied an ordinary image, and then printed the same image over and again! When asked why he had repeated his image of a soup can 100 times, Warhol simply replied that he really liked the soup!

Pop art is meant to be fun. It's interesting to make an everyday image, like this handprint, into colorful art.

ANDY WARHOL

See if you can produce your own Andy Warhol-inspired art. Warhol repeated a black and white image of Marilyn Monroe. He colored it using a technique known as **screen printing**. In screen-printing, the design is separated into several colors. A **stencil** is made for each color, and the paint is applied one color at a time.

CREATE IT!

You will need: a photograph, a photocopier or scanner and printer, watercolor paints, a sponge, printer paper, a pencil, masking tape, scissors, an adult to help

1 Find a photograph of yourself, or maybe a famous person who you like. Photocopy or scan and print out the photograph twice in black and white.

2 Decide which areas you want to be which color. To make your stencils, hold a photocopy up to a window. Trace each area onto a different sheet of printer paper. Simple shapes are best.

dark areas

t-shirt

skin color

background

3 Ask an adult to help you cut around each stencil. You want the hole to be the area you paint. It can help to shade the area you need to cut out.

4 Using masking tape, secure the skin color stencil in place first. Carefully paint the area. Don't let the brush creep under the stencil. Once dry, do the other stencils in turn.

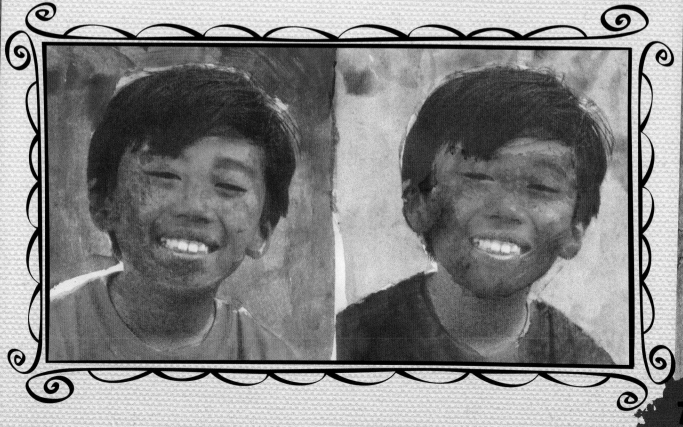

ANDY WARHOL

AUGUST 6, 1928
FEBRUARY 22, 1987

Fans sometimes leave gifts at Andy Warhol's grave, near Pittsburgh. Many leave cans of tomato soup because of Warhol's famous soup can painting!

CREATE IT!

You will need: paper, a pencil, colored pencils

1 Draw your soup can using a pencil. To draw the **cylinder** shape, first draw a flattened oval near the top of your paper. Next, draw two parallel lines down each side of the oval. At the bottom of the can, draw an arc shape that is the same shape as the bottom half of your oval.

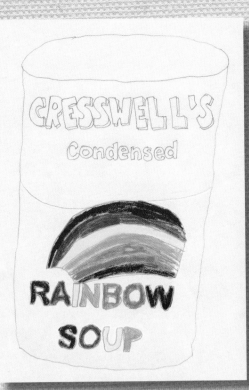

CRESSWELL'S
Condensed

2 Start to decorate your can. Add the name and flavor of your soup. If you have a computer and printer you can use, you could print out the words and trace them.

3 Finish coloring in your can. Add some oval lines on the lid.

4 You could photocopy your can art and make a Warhol-style repeat pattern, like the one below.

ROY LICHTENSTEIN

Most of Roy Lichtenstein's best-known works are close, but not exact, copies of comic book illustrations. He painted the images onto large **canvases**. Not everyone liked his work. In 1964, an article in *Life* magazine asked if Lichtenstein was "the worst artist in the US"!

TECHNIQUE TIPS

Ben-Day dots were used in comic book illustrations in the 1950s and 1960s. Lichtenstein used Ben-Day dots in his illustrations. Instead of using printed sheets of dots, like a printer would have done, he carefully painted each dot onto his canvas! At first he used a dog-grooming brush dipped in paint to make the dots! Later, he used metal screens or handmade stencils.

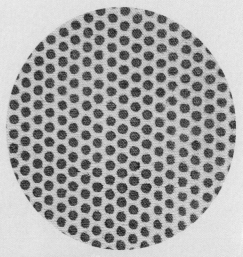

CREATE IT!

You will need: some graph paper, a pencil, markers, colored pencils

1 Draw your picture on the graph paper. The dots will be the size of a square, so make sure you draw your picture large enough so there are plenty of dots in each shape.

2 Color in your shapes. Use Ben-Day dots to fill some areas. Color other areas in solid color. Use colored pencil to add a background to some areas.

3 When you have finished coloring in, go over the outlines of your drawing using a black marker. Color in your comic book style writing, too.

CREATE IT!

You will need: colored paper, thin white cardboard, a pencil, an eraser, scissors, glue, poster paint, a paintbrush, a black marker

1 Using a pencil, draw a large explosion shape on some bright colored paper. Cut it out and glue it onto a different, brightly colored sheet of paper.

2 Write your word in capital letters on the cardboard. Outline your letters so the word becomes a solid shape.

3 Using a black marker, go over the outline of your word. Erase the old pencil lines.

4 Carefully paint the inside of your word using a bright color.

5 Using a pencil, draw an outline around your word shape. Make the outline the same distance from the word all the way around. This will be the line you cut along when you cut out your shape.

6 Cut out your word using your pencil outline as a guide. Glue it in place on your background.

ROBERT RAUSCHENBERG

Robert Rauschenberg was an American artist. He created **collages** using newspaper cuttings and paint. He collected trash and objects he found on the street and used them in his artwork, too.

Rauschenberg was both a painter and a sculptor and he liked to mix the two skills to make sculptures he called "combines."

TECHNIQUE TIPS

Rauschenberg made his collages using house paint. He used techniques such as painting using a tire dipped in ink! Rauschenberg liked to use objects he found in his art because they were things that he could not have made himself. He also liked the surprise of not knowing what he would find.

CREATE IT!

You will need: poster paints, a paintbrush, thick paper or cardboard, glue, some old newspapers and magazines

1 Rip up pages from a newspaper and glue them onto your sheet of paper.

2 Choose some photographs from color magazines and glue them in place.

3 Paint some areas of your collage. Draw some dashed lines and shapes, too. Perhaps add color to some of the black and white photographs using a thin coat of paint.

CREATE IT!

Rauschenberg's "combine" sculptures (right) use a mixture of found objects and paint. Make one yourself.

You will need: poster paint, colored paper, a collection of objects, an adult

1 Ask an adult to help you select your objects. You want to be sure you are allowed to use them, and that they are safe.

A stamp showing Rauschenberg's *Monogram*, a stuffed goat and car tire sculpture

2 Paint some of your objects in bright colors.

3 Paint a colorful background on thick colored paper. You can either stand your sculpture on the paper or place the paper behind it.

4 Start to put your sculpture together. Use your imagination. It can be as crazy as you like! Think of a name for your finished work. What would you call this one?

CLAES OLDENBURG

Claes Oldenburg is best known for making enormous replicas of everyday objects. He has made giant hamburgers, and cake slices out of vinyl filled with stuffing. In the 1980s a company in Los Angeles asked architect Frank Gehry to design them a creative-looking office. Gehry asked Oldenburg for help, and designed this amazing oversized binocular building!

Oldenburg's binocular building

18

You will need: paints, a paintbrush, thick paper or cardboard, white chalk, modeling clay

1 Paint a gray road onto a piece of cardboard. Once the paint is dry add some white lines with chalk.

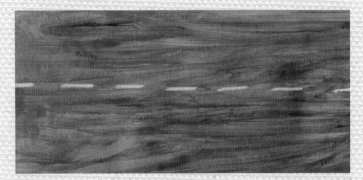

2 Create some houses and trees using modeling clay.

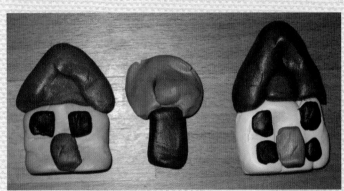

We made a giant beach ball house. What will you make?

CREATE IT!

You will need: newspaper, masking tape, printer paper, poster paint, a handful of rice, glue

1 Scrunch up several sheets of newspaper until you have enough to make a large circle.

2 Wrap a large sheet of newspaper around your newspaper balls. Make it into a hamburger bun shape and secure with masking tape. Repeat steps 1 and 2 so you have two newspaper hamburger buns.

3 Using smaller newspaper balls, make another slightly larger but flatter newspaper shape. This will be your hamburger patty.

4 Paint your newspaper patty in different shades of brown. Paint the hamburger buns in a pale yellowy brown color.

5 Paint a sheet of printer paper in shades of light green. Once the paint is dry rip the paper into large pieces.

6 Put all your hamburger pieces together. Glue some rice on top to look like sesame seeds.

PATRICK CAULFIELD

Patrick Caulfield was an English Pop art painter and printmaker. He painted simple household objects and **interiors**. He used flat, bold colors in his paintings, with shapes outlined in black. Caulfield did not paint any detail, he liked to paint simple shapes.

Art in the style of Caulfield

CREATE IT!

You will need: a pencil, a paintbrush, thick paper, an eraser, a black marker, poster paints

1 Draw your design onto paper using pencil. Try to overlap your objects.

2 Using an eraser, rub away any overlapping lines that you don't need.

3 Paint your picture using bright, solid colors.

TECHNIQUE TIPS

Caulfield used house paint or **acrylic** paint. To create a flat color using poster paint, use a large, soft brush. When your paint is starting to dry, go over it very lightly with a dry brush to blend your brushstrokes.

4 Once your paint is dry, draw around the outlines using a black marker.

DAVID HOCKNEY

David Hockney is well known for his series of paintings of Los Angeles swimming pools. He often paints beautiful ripples in the water.

Hockney also creates photo collages, using photographs of the same image but from different angles. He calls these photo collages "joiners." More recently, Hockney has begun to use computer tablets to produce his art!

A portrait of David Hockney done on a tablet by artist Florent Bonnefoi

TECHNIQUE TIPS

Hockney used acrylic paint on canvas to create his swimming pool paintings. An easier way to achieve the same water ripple effect is to use a white crayon or candle to draw the ripples. When you brush watercolor paint over the crayon it **resists** the paint and stays white.

CREATE IT!

You will need: thick white paper, a white crayon or candle, colored crayons, watercolor paint, a paintbrush

1 Draw your swimmers using crayons. Draw your ripples in white crayon. It is hard to see the white crayon marks. You could make little pencil marks at the side of your paper to remember where you have drawn each line.

2 Paint over your crayon drawing with watercolor. The white ripples and swimmers will show through.

3 Use a mix of blue and green paints to make a realistic, shimmering swimming pool.

CREATE IT!

You will need: magazine photographs or your own photographs, scissors, thick paper or cardboard, glue, a breadboard

1 Find a couple of photos of the same scene from different angles if you can. Make sure they are photos that it will be OK to cut up.

2 Cut each photo into around 12 pieces.

3 Rearrange the pieces of photograph so you mix the two angles. Move them around on your paper until you are happy with your collage.

4 You will need to glue the pieces at the back down first. To do this, place a breadboard over your collage. Place your hand under your paper and carefully turn the paper and breadboard over.

5 Carefully lift off the paper. Your pieces will be upside down but in the right position. Dab glue onto the backs of the pieces and press your paper back in place. Once dry, turn the paper over and stick down any loose corners.

RICHARD HAMILTON

Richard Hamilton was an English painter and collage artist. His 1956 collage *Just what is it that makes today's homes so different, so appealing?* is believed to be the earliest Pop art piece.

Hamilton believed Pop art must be popular, easily forgotten, low-cost, mass-produced, aimed at youth, and be amusing, **gimmicky**, **glamorous**, and big business!

TECHNIQUE TIPS

Hamilton was inspired by images in newspapers, magazines, and advertisements. He worked using photocopies and photographs, cutting and changing the images' sizes to create his collages.

CREATE IT!

Create a Hamilton collage. We have used 1950s photographs, but you could create a really modern version instead.

You will need: old magazines, scissors, cardboard, glue

1 Cut out some pictures of people, objects, and room interiors. Remember to make your collage witty and glamorous!

2 Arrange your images until you are happy with your collage and glue them in place.

GLOSSARY

acrylic A fast-drying paint containing an acrylic substance.

art critics People who write their opinions about art.

brands Goods identified as the product of a single maker by a printed mark.

canvases Pieces of cloth used as a surface for painting.

collages Works of art made by gluing pieces of different materials to a flat surface.

cylinder A shape made up of two parallel circles of identical size and shape and a curved surface that completely connects their borders

gimmicky Using a trick or device to attract business or attention.

glamorous Excitingly attractive.

inspiration Something that stimulates an artist to be creative.

interiors The internal or inner part of something, such as the inside of a house.

mass-produced Produced in quantity usually by machinery.

resists Withstands the effect of something.

screen printing Forcing ink or paint onto a surface through a prepared screen of fine material so as to create a picture or pattern.

stencil A piece of material with a design that is cut out and through which ink or paint is forced onto a surface to be printed.

FURTHER INFORMATION

Books

Anderson, Kirsten. *Who Was Andy Warhol?*, New York, NY: Grosset & Dunlap, 2014.

Sipperley, Keli. *A Look at Pop Art (Art and Music)*, Vero Beach, FL: Rourke Educational Media, 2014.

Websites
Tate Gallery site with information, and a project idea for children:
http://www.tate.org.uk/learn/online-resources/glossary/p/pop-art

https://kids.tate.org.uk/create/pop_art_hat.shtm

Ducksters site with information on Pop art and artists:
http://www.ducksters.com/history/art/pop_art.php

Publisher's note to educators and parents:
Our editors have carefully reviewed these websites to ensure that they are suitable for students. Many websites change frequently, however, and we cannot guarantee that a site's future contents will continue to meet our high standards of quality and educational value. Be advised that students should be closely supervised whenever they access the Internet.